# WEST COUNTRY ENGLISH

**Cornwall – Devon – Somerset - Dorset**

Compiled by Graeme Davis

**ABSON BOOKS LONDON**

5 Sidney Square London E1 2EY
Tel 020 7790 4737
Fax 020 7790 7346
email absonbooks@aol.com
web www.absonbooks.co.uk

**ABSON BOOKS LONDON**
First published June 2008
© Graeme Davis
Design by Creative Mouse Ltd
Cover photo by John Lilley

Printed by
Guttenberg Press, Malta
ISBN 978 0902920 811

# INTRODUCTION

The Wurzels sent it up (*ooh aar, ooh aar ay*), and the image of the turnip-eating and cider-drinking West Country yokel has become a staple of comedy. Yet the dialect of England's West Country remains today a form of expression distinctive of its people and evocative of its landscapes. West Country English is still very much alive, more so than any other dialect of the British Isles save possibly Lowland Scots. People in the West Country really do use words included in this glossary while visitors to the area can appreciate the richness of expression and gentle sounds of this vibrant, rural tongue.

The words in this glossary have a wide distribution in the counties of Cornwall, Devon, Somerset and Dorset, with the exception of a handful that are found mainly in west Cornwall and the Isles of Scilly and mostly derive from the Celtic Cornish language (these are marked with an asterisk). Many of the words in this dictionary are found also in Gloucestershire, Wiltshire and the urban dialect of Bristol.

\* Mainly used in west Cornwall and the Isles of Scilly

| | |
|---|---|
| **a-** | prefix to many verbs, indicating a thoroughness or completion of an action, as *a-vroze*–completely frozen, *a-made* – made up |
| **aar** | yes |
| **abroad** | anywhere away from here, which can be as close as the next town |
| **acker** | friend, as *Acker Bilk* the jazz legend and clarinet player |
| **acker, hacker** | two-clawed tool used for digging *teddies* |
| **aigs** | eggs |
| **aish** | ash tree |
| **ale-up** | earth-up potatoes |
| **allow** | believe |
| **angle-titch** | earthworm, a fidget. |
| **anguish** | inflammation |
| **ankicher** | handkerchief |
| **ansum** | friend |
| **anywhen** | at any time |

| | |
|---|---|
| **appledrone, appledrain, applebee** | wasp |
| **arg** | argue |
| **arsy-varsy** | upside down, other way round |
| **a-thirt** | across |
| **avore** | before |
| **ay** | yes (rhymes with *hay*) |
| **ay?** | pardon? |

**B**

| | |
|---|---|
| **backalong** | previously |
| **backhouse** | outhouse |
| **bad** | ill |
| **baird** | bird |
| **baisly** | dirty (see **cabby**) |
| **bullyrag** | tell off, scold, swear at |

| | |
|---|---|
| **barton** | farm-yard |
| **bastick** | basket |
| **batch** | hillock |
| **beast** | farm animal, cow |
| **becall** | deride |
| **beens** | because |
| **begayed** | bewitched |
| **begrumpled** | offended |
| **bettering** | improvement in health |
| **belong to do** | usually do, as *I don't belong to do that* |
| **belve** | animal bellow |
| **betwaddled** | befuddled by drink |
| **between the two lights** | between sunset and moon-rise |
| **bibber** | shiver |
| **biddle** | beetle, to grow bigger |
| **bissle** | grubby, dirty, make dirty |
| **bissly** | something unpleasant, unpleasant surprise |

| | |
|---|---|
| **bist the?** | are you? |
| **bit-an-drap** | meal |
| **biver** | shake, shiver |
| **blad** | idiot |
| **blunk** | snow |
| **bobbish** | in good health |
| **bottom** | valley |
| **boughten** | shop-bought, ready-made food |
| **braid** | bread |
| **brantitus** | bronchitis |
| **brave** | fit, well, in good health |
| **brish** | brush |
| **bugger** | non-offensive swear word, as *running empty buggered* – O bother, it's completely broken |
| **bullies** | pebbles * |
| **bullums** | sloes, blackthorn fruits |
| **Burdgwater** | Bridgewater |
| **buster** | streaming cold, child full of mischief |

| | |
|---|---|
| **C** **cabby** | dirty (see **baisly**) |
| **caddle** | muddle |
| **cakey** | feeble-minded |
| **call home** | remember something, announce marriage bans |
| **cancervells** | icicles (see **tinklebobs**) |
| **carr** | carry, particularly a coffin, hence to bury, as *he was carried to church* |
| **canvas** | linoleum or vinyl flooring |
| **caudle** | messy, to sweep the dust under the carpet. |
| **caunce** | flag stone, or yard floored with flag stones * |
| **chacks** | cheeks |
| **chad** | gorse |
| **chattermag** | gossip |
| **cheens** | potato sprouts |
| **cherks** | cinders |
| **chetterlings** | entrails of a pig |
| **chibbles, chippols** | spring onions |
| **child** | girl child, as *is it a boy or a child?* |

| | |
|---|---|
| **chill** | warm, as *I've chilled the oven* |
| **chillurn** | children |
| **chimley** | chimney |
| **chimp** | break the shoots off potatoes |
| **chitterpie** | magpie, chatterbox |
| **chuff** | happy |
| **chuff as** | |
| **a maggot** | miserable |
| **chug-chug** | used to call pigs to their food |
| **chuggy pig** | child's word for a pig, also a snapdragon and a woodlouse |
| **chump** | large log, piece of firewood |
| **churchtown** | group of houses surrounding a church, the village centre |
| **chuting** | guttering (sounds like shooting) |
| **claggy** | heavy soil |
| **clavy** | mantelpiece |
| **clicky** | left-handed * (elsewhere *skiffy*) |
| **cluck** | broody hen |

| | |
|---|---|
| **clunker** | windpipe |
| **coll** | embrace |
| **combe** | deep valley |
| **come-by-chance** | illegitimate child (see **gatepost child**) |
| **conkerbell** | icicle |
| **coose** | a gossip * |
| **coupie down** | crouch down |
| **cow-baby** | coward |
| **cowlease** | unmown field |
| **cradlehood** | infancy |
| **creen up** | complain about being ill |
| **crams** | lies, as *pack of crams* |
| **crowst** | a lunch eaten in the fields, a picnic * |
| **culver** | pigeon, wood-pigeon |
| **cut up** | talk in Standard English instead of one's usual West Country English |
| **cuzzel** | soft * |

**D**

| | |
|---|---|
| dabbered up | mud-spattered |
| dabster | expert |
| dadder | bewilder |
| dagging | longing |
| Darset | Dorset |
| dashels | thistles |
| davered | faded, particularly flowers |
| Debn | Devon |
| dewbit | breakfast |
| dew-snail | slug |
| didikai | gypsy |
| dido | noise row, disturbance |
| dimity | dark |
| dimpsy | summer twilight, as *getting a bit dimpsy* |
| dinky | tiny |
| ditch | bank, earth thrown up when digging a ditch |
| dite | small child |
| doan'ee | don't you |

| | |
|---|---|
| **dollop** | lump of, large portion of |
| **doughboy** | dumpling |
| **doxy** | dainty, petite |
| **doxy-maid** | flirt |
| **drackly** | immediately, in a minute, soon, some time |
| **drang** | passageway between two walls |
| **drashel** | threshold |
| **dreckly** | soon but not right now, as *I'll come dreckly* |
| **drong** | narrow passage |
| **duckish** | dark, dull |
| **dummets** | twilight |
| **durn** | door frame |

| | | |
|---|---|---|
| **E** | each | everybody, as *goodnight each* |
| | easement | relief |
| | ees | yes |
| | **Eggseckerter, Exegeter** | Exeter, one of many West Country expansions of place names, as *Illfrackombee,* Ilfracombe |
| | emmet | ant or other insect or small animal, as *four-legged emmet,* a newt. Also a visitor to the West Country or tourist (insult) (see **evet**) |
| | enting down | pouring with rain |
| | eve | become wet with condensation |
| | evet | newt |

| | | |
|---|---|---|
| **F** | fagot | bundle of wood |
| | fantod | fuss |
| | fardle, faddle | something which is carried, as *pack and fardle,* bag and baggage |

| | |
|---|---|
| **ferrick about** | search, also fuss around |
| **figgety-pudden** | plum pudding |
| **fightable** | argumentative, pugnacious |
| **fledged & flied** | said of children who have grown up and left the parental home |
| **footy** | insignificant |
| **forceput** | emergency |
| **foreside back** | back to front |
| **forthy** | cheeky |
| **frame up** | square up for a fight |
| **freck** | fuss |
| **French nut** | walnut |
| **frightened** | surprised |
| **full as an egg** | weather which is ready to storm |
| **full of it** | full of mischief |

**G**

| | |
|---|---|
| gad | stake |
| gaddle | gulp, drink fast |
| gake, gawk | look, stare |
| gramfer, granfer | grandfather |
| gammer, grammer | grandmother |
| gamut | nonsense |
| gatepost child | illegitimate child (see **come by chance**) |
| gert | big |
| get 'ome do! | wake up, think about it! |
| gidgy | a trick |
| gifts | white spots on fingernails, believed to foretell receipt of a gift |
| gill-cup | buttercup |
| giss on! | don't talk rubbish! |
| givish | generous |
| gockey | idiot * |
| goc | cuckoo |

| | |
|---|---|
| **God's pussycat** | furry caterpillar |
| **goin' home fast** | dying |
| **gone in** | nearly dead |
| **goo-coos** | bluebells |
| **goosegog** | gooseberry |
| **gravy** | sweat, as *hard work makes the gravy run* |
| **greybird** | thrush |
| **grockle, gockle** | tourist, holiday maker – polite alternative to *emmet* |
| **grockle-grappling** | term used by *Search and Rescue* in the village of Culdrose to mean rescuing tourists from a watery grave |
| **groushans** | dregs of tea * |
| **gurt, girt** | great, big, large, heavy |
| **gwain** | going |
| **gwidgee-gwee** | blister * |

| | |
|---|---|
| hag-rode | bewitched |
| haling | coughing |
| hammered | drunk (see **zidered up**) |
| handsome | pleasant, fine. Also *me old handsome,* my old mate |
| hay | fence, hedge, enclosed place, homestead |
| he | it, as *put he down there* |
| hedgyboar | hedgehog |
| helling | roof * |
| hilts and gilts | piglets, the hilts are female and the gilts male. |
| hinkypunk | will o' the wisp, spirit that misleads travellers. |
| hoboo | child's word for a horse |
| hossifer | officer |
| housing | gossiping from house to house |
| how? | why? |
| huppenstop | raised stone platform outside a farm where milk churns were once left for collection |
| hurted | hurt |

## I

| | |
|---|---|
| **I** | me, as *look at ee lookin at I* |
| **injin** | engine |

## J

| | |
|---|---|
| **jag** | snag |
| **janner** | Plymouth word for someone who makes their living from the sea |
| **jasper** | wasp |
| **jig, make a** | make a mockery of something |
| **jine** | join |
| **Johnny Fortnight** | itinerant peddler |
| **jollop** | medicine |
| **joney** | mantelpiece ornament, particularly a Staffordshire flat back |
| **joppety-joppety** | nervous anxiety |
| **jowder** | fish seller |

**K**

| | |
|---|---|
| keep | cattle fodder |
| kiddly | milk sops, soft food for an invalid |
| Kimberling | someone from Weymouth in Dorset |
| kitting | stealing |
| kitty bags | leggings, traditionally bags wrapped around labourers' legs |
| knap | knoll, rising ground |

**L**

| | |
|---|---|
| labbet | drudge |
| lacing | hiding, beating |
| lam | hit, as *I'll lam thee* |
| larry, larr | fit of laziness, as *I got the larry* |
| leak | drop, as *a leak of tea* |
| leary, leery | faint from hunger |

| | |
|---|---|
| **leat** | water channel, mill race |
| **leet** | little |
| **lem** | eleven |
| **lent lilies** | daffodils |
| **lewth** | a shelter from the wind |
| **ling** | throw * |
| **linney** | shed |
| **litsome** | cheerful |
| **litter** | confusion |
| **long family** | large family |
| **long-headed** | wise |
| **long-tailed rabbit** | poached pheasant (rabbit shooting is legal, but not pheasant shooting without a licence) |
| **loony** | rooster |
| **lost** | lose |
| **love-lay** | lovely |
| **lumpy** | heavy |

# M

| | |
|---|---|
| madderdo'ee? | does it matter? |
| maggoty | fanciful |
| maid | daughter, girl, particularly an unmarried daughter |
| make hay sweet | kiss and cuddle in a hayfield |
| mang | mix |
| mangelwurzel | type of turnip used mainly as cattle feed |
| mazed | angry |
| meat | food, to feed, as *to meat the pigs* |
| meat beans | broad beans |
| mebbe | maybe |
| me ansum, me handsome, me luvver | mate, friend - all forms of address |
| miff | minor quarrel |
| milky-dashels, milky-dashless, musky-dashles | rabbit food, particularly dandelion leaves |
| mind | remember |
| mixen | dung heap |

| | |
|---|---|
| **montious** | very, as *montious gert thing* |
| **moory** | low-lying damp ground |
| **moot** | tree root or tree stump |
| **mucker** | friend, as *me ole mucker* |
| **muryan** | ant, hard worker * |
| **mushelroom** | mushroom |

## N

| | |
|---|---|
| **nammet** | lunch |
| **near** | mean, miserly |
| **nesh** | tender |
| **niceys** | sweets |
| **nirrup** | donkey |
| **nottlin** | cold |
| **nubbie** | bun, particularly a plain bun |
| **nuddick** | neck |
| **nuff** | enough |

**O**

| | |
|---|---|
| **Oh Lawky!** | O God! |
| **on the sniff** | suspicious, looking out for something |
| **Ooh arr** | I see, okay, yes, is that so? Intonation may convey the meaning intended, or may not |
| **ood** | wood |
| **oozle** | throat, as *wet yer oozle* - have a drink |
| **orts** | left over food |
| **overlook** | bewitch |
| **over-right** | opposite |

**P**

| | |
|---|---|
| pank | pant |
| parish lantern | moon |
| peeth | well * |
| penny-liggan | penniless, out of pocket |
| pelt | anger |
| perp | sulk |
| pick in | bring in washing from a line |
| pindy | mouldy |
| pinnicking | puny, weak |
| pinsle | pimple |
| pisky | pixie, as *laughing like a pisky,* drunk |
| pisky laid | pixie led, lost |
| pisky ridden | accident prone |
| please? | pardon? (Not heard) |
| plim | swell |
| plum | prove bread dough |

| | |
|---|---|
| **plush** | cut a hedge down almost to the ground |
| **popple** | pebble |
| **poppy** | foxglove (foxglove flowers can be popped) |
| **punkie night** | Halloween |

**Q**

| | |
|---|---|
| **quilkin** | frog * |
| **quob** | quiver, shiver |

| **R** | **race** | a string of beads, arrange in a row, particularly plum-stones on the edge of a plate |
|---|---|---|
| | **ratch** | stretch |
| | **rathe** | early |
| | **raw milk** | full cream milk |
| | **ream** | single cream |
| | **red-dick** | robin |
| | **reeve** | unravel |
| | **riptackle** | tomboy |
| | **rory-tory** | bright, colourful, particularly of clothes |
| | **ruckle** | peat stack, as on Somerset Levels |
| | **ruff** | roof |
| | **rusty** | rancid, particularly of bacon |

| | |
|---|---|
| **sassy** | impudent |
| **scag** | to scratch on brambles or barbed wire |
| **scat** | a beat in music |
| **scollard** | student |
| **scruff** | fight, particularly children in play |
| **scrumpy** | strong cider |
| **scrumpy & western** | comical folk-style songs delivered in West Country English |
| **scud** | scab on a wound |
| **shacklen** | loose limbed |
| **shaking up** | approaching, as *he's shaking up ninety* |
| **sight** | number or quantity |
| **skews I** | excuse me |
| **skiffy** | left-handed |
| **skimmish** | squeamish |
| **skimpings** | grit used on icy roads |
| **slock** | entice |

| | |
|---|---|
| **smeech, smitch** | smoke, cloud of dust |
| **snicker** | door, *shut snicker* - shut the door |
| **some** | very, as *some funny* |
| **somewhen** | sometime - but don't hold your breath |
| **spuddling** | struggling |
| **spurticles** | spectacles |
| **stagged** | stuck in mud, behind with work |
| **stay-stomach** | elevenses or other snack |
| **steeved** | frozen |
| **stram** | stride |
| **stroathing** | hurrying * |
| **stuggy** | stocky |

| | |
|---|---|
| **T** | |
| **tacker** | toddler, child |
| **taffety** | dainty, picky in eating |
| **taffle** | tangle |
| **tap** | sole of a boot also to repair a boot |
| **tay** | tea |
| **teave** | struggle |
| **teddies,**<br>**teddy oggies** | potatoes, particularly small potatoes |
| **teddy-fat weather** | damp & warm weather which encourages potatoes to grow |
| **teddy-hoggy** | potato pasty |
| **te-geddle-brauth,**<br>**tea-kettle-broth** | bread in milk, usually with butter, salt & pepper |
| **tel** | talk |
| **thirl** | thin, hungry |
| **thunder**<br>**& lightning** | bread spread with golden syrup and cream |

| | |
|---|---|
| **tilty** | peevish |
| **tinklebobs** | icicles (see **cancervells**) |
| **tiss-toss** | head over heals, turn somersaults |
| **tom-toddy** | tadpole |
| **travelling** | walking |
| **turmit** | turnip |
| **twankleten** | melancholy |
| **twite** | reproach |

## U

| | |
|---|---|
| **ugs pudding** | pork sausage |
| **undercreepen** | sly, hypocritical |
| **upright twelve** | exactly twelve midnight or midday |
| **urch** | rich |
| **urd** | red |
| **urts** | whortleberries, bilberries |
| **us** | we |

**V**

| | |
|---|---|
| vall | autumn |
| vall (to) | begin |
| vamp | pour tea into a half-empty cup, top-up |
| varmer | farmer, especially as a form of address |
| vearns | bracken, but sometimes used for fern |
| vencrake | corn crake |
| versey | read the Bible verse-by-verse |
| vitty | proper |
| vlam-new | brand new |
| vlinders | splinters |
| vorenoon | morning |
| vorrin parts | foreign parts, anywhere east or north of Bristol |
| vower | four |
| vroze | frozen |
| vuzz | gorse |
| vuzz-peg | hedgehog |

# W

| | |
|---|---|
| **wants** | moles, spots |
| **westar** | western |
| **whicker** | neigh |
| **whist** | a sty or eye inflammation |
| **wimwam** | fancy, fad |
| **withywind** | bindweed |
| **wopsey** | wasp |
| **wrack** | consequence |
| **writ** | wrote |
| **wurzelspeak** | parody of West Country English |

**Y**

| | |
|---|---|
| **yaffer** | heifer |
| **yan** | first number in a shepherd's counting rhyme. (*yan, tan, tethera, methera, pip, sethera, wineberry, wagtail, tarrydiddle, den*). Versions are found throughout England & this Cornish version is very like the Lake District form. |
| **yarbs** | herbs |
| **yark** | make ready |
| **yetties** | residents of Yetminster, Dorset |
| **yokel** | West Country resident |
| **yoller** | yellow |
| **yongan** | young man or woman, form of address as *alright youngan?* |
| **yop** | talk quickly |

## Z

| | |
|---|---|
| zackly | exactly |
| zam-zawd | stewed tea |
| zam-zoodled | overcooked food |
| zartain | certain |
| zat | soft |
| zeale | sack |
| zider | cider |
| zidered up | drunk (see **hammered**) |
| zlatter | scatter |
| zummerleaze | unmown grass for summer feed |
| Zummerzet | Somerset |
| zummat | something |
| zwail | swagger |
| zweal | scorch |

# IDIOMS

**alright me ansum?** – how are you doing, old friend?
**alright me luvver?** – alright mate?
**belly like a Barnstaple man, bum like a Barnstaple maid** – fat
**daft as a carrot half scraped** – daft as a brush
**like a hen with one chick** – with a one-track mind
**mazed as a brish** – daft as a brush
**mazed as a curlew** – raving mad
**mazed as a sheep** – a bit thick
**'ow be nackin vore?** – How are you?
**'ow bist 'ee?** – how are you? (a greeting)
**pick the washing** – get the washing in off the line
**thirsty as a gull** – ready for some zider
**wash your feet** – paddle in the sea
**way back along** – years ago
**where's that to?** – Where's that?

# OTHER TITLES AVAILABLE

**Language Glossaries**
American English/English American
Australian English/English Australian
Cumbrian English
Gay slang
Geordie English
Hip Hop English
Home Counties English
Irish English/English Irish
Lancashire English
Military Slang
Playground Slang & Teenspeak
Prison Slang
Rhyming Cockney Slang
Rude Rhyming Slang
Scottish English/English Scottish
Scouse English

West Country English
Yiddish English/English Yiddish
Yorkshire English

**History**
The Death of Kings – A history
of how the Kings & Queens of
England died

**Literary Quiz & Puzzle Books**

| | |
|---|---|
| Jane Austen | Gilbert & Sullivan |
| Bronte Sisters | Thomas Hardy |
| Shakespeare | |

All of these titles area available from good booksellers
or by contacting the publisher:
Abson Books London 5 Sidney Square London E1 2EY
Tel 020 7790 4737 Fax 020 7790 7346
email absonbooks@aol.com
web www.absonbooks.co.uk